TIME
FOR KIDS

W9-ART-035

SUPER SCIENCE KIT

PRODUCED BY

DOWNTOWN
BOOKWORKS INC.

PRESIDENT: Julie Merberg
EDITORIAL DIRECTOR: Sarah Parvis
SENIOR CONTRIBUTORS: Patricia Janes, Allyson Kulavis, Susan Perry, Renée Skelton, Jenny Tesar
SPECIAL THANKS: Patty Brown, Matt Shay, Barbara Gogan, Heather Lockwood Hughes, Stephen Callahan, Liz Reitman, Sana Hong

DESIGNED BY
Brian Michael Thomas/Our Hero Productions

ILLUSTRATIONS BY
Darin Anderson/Shay Design

Experiment Development: Lindsay Milner, Evelyn Tsang, Elke Steinwender, Sharon King-Majaury
Mad Science® is on a mission to spark the imagination and curiosity of children everywhere. We provide fun, interactive, educational programs that instill a clear understanding of what science is really about and how it affects the world around us. Visit www.madscience.org to find a location near you!

PUBLISHER: Bob Der
MANAGING EDITOR, TIME For Kids MAGAZINE: Nellie Gonzalez Cutler
EDITOR, TIME LEARNING VENTURES: Jonathan Rosenbloom

PUBLISHER: Richard Fraiman
VICE PRESIDENT, BUSINESS DEVELOPMENT & STRATEGY: Steven Sandonato
EXECUTIVE DIRECTOR, MARKETING SERVICES: Carol Pittard
EXECUTIVE DIRECTOR, RETAIL & SPECIAL SALES: Tom Mifsud
EXECUTIVE PUBLISHING DIRECTOR: Joy Butts
EDITORIAL DIRECTOR: Stephen Koepp
EDITORIAL OPERATIONS DIRECTOR: Michael Q. Bullerdick
DIRECTOR, BOOKAZINE DEVELOPMENT & MARKETING: Laura Adam
FINANCE DIRECTOR: Glenn Buonocore
ASSOCIATE PUBLISHING DIRECTOR: Megan Pearlman
ASSISTANT GENERAL COUNSEL: Helen Wan
ASSISTANT DIRECTOR, SPECIAL SALES: Ilene Schreider
DESIGN & PREPRESS MANAGER: Anne-Michelle Gallero
BRAND MANAGER: Jonathan White
ASSOCIATE PREPRESS MANAGER: Alex Voznesenskiy
ASSOCIATE PRODUCTION MANAGER: Kimberly Marshall
ASSISTANT BRAND MANAGER: Stephanie Braga

SPECIAL THANKS: Christine Austin, Jeremy Biloon, Alex Borinstein, Jim Childs, Susan Chodakiewicz, Rose Cirrincione, Lauren Hall Clark, Jacqueline Fitzgerald, Christine Font, Jenna Goldberg, David Kahn, Suzanne Janso, Raphael Joa, Jeffrey Kaji, Mona Li, Amy Mangus, Robert Marasco, Amy Migliaccio, Georgia Millman-Perlah, Nina Mistry, Myles Ringel, Dave Rozzelle, Sasha Shapiro, Soren Shapiro, Adriana Tierno, Emily Wheeler, Vanessa Wu

For information on TIME For Kids magazine for the classroom or home, go to TIMEFORKIDS.COM or call 1-800-777-8600.

Published by TIME For Kids Books, an imprint of Time Home Entertainment Inc.
135 West 50th Street
New York, New York 10020

ISBN 10: 1-61893-012-5
ISBN 13: 978-1-61893-012-5

TIME For Kids is a trademark of Time Inc.

We welcome your comments and suggestions about TIME For Kids Books. Please write to us at:

TIME For Kids BOOKS
ATTENTION: BOOK EDITORS
P.O. BOX 11016
DES MOINES, IA 50336-1016

If you would like to order any of our TIME For Kids or SI Kids hardcover Collector's Edition books, please call us at 1-800-327-6388 (Monday through Friday, 7:00 a.m.–8:00 p.m., or Saturday, 7:00 a.m.–6:00 p.m. Central Time).

PRODUCED BY
becker&mayer!, LLC.
11120 NE 33rd Place, Suite 101
Bellevue, WA 98004
www.beckermayer.com

PROJECT MANAGEMENT BY
Delia Greve
BOX DESIGN BY
Sarah Baynes
PRODUCTION MANAGEMENT BY
Jennifer Marx

1 BKM 12

CONTENTS

 Experiments marked with a green test tube can be set up and performed in less than one hour.

 Experiments marked with a yellow flask can be completed in a matter of hours.

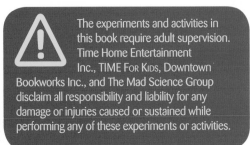 Experiments marked with a red beaker will take more than a day to complete. See individual experiments for time requirements.

 The experiments and activities in this book require adult supervision. Time Home Entertainment Inc., TIME For Kids, Downtown Bookworks Inc., and The Mad Science Group disclaim all responsibility and liability for any damage or injuries caused or sustained while performing any of these experiments or activities.

WHAT DO SCIENTISTS DO?

Scientists observe, study, look for patterns, and try to find general rules to explain how things work or why things happen. A scientific law describes something that has been observed many times. Understanding these rules often helps scientists create or improve processes that we use in our world every day. The laws of gravity, for example, explain why we stick to the Earth instead of floating away.

The Scientific Method

Scientists follow a set of steps called the scientific method. They begin by making observations that lead to generalizations about why an event happens. These "first guess" generalizations are called **hypotheses.** Scientists test a hypothesis many times to make sure a certain outcome is not an accident or a fluke. As scientists test a hypothesis and observe the results of experiments, they look for evidence to support a hypothesis. If they can support the hypothesis, it may lead to a theory or a law of science.

All scientists use six basic skills in the scientific method: observing, communicating, classifying, measuring, inferring, and predicting.

A paleontologist is a type of scientist who studies the remains of organisms that lived long ago.

OBSERVING We use our senses to get information about the world around us. We can also use tools, such as microscopes, magnifying glasses, and telescopes. Scientists do not include opinions in their observations. They only record what they observe.

COMMUNICATING Scientists share observations, discoveries, and results in many ways. They write, draw, and use visual aids such as graphs, charts, maps, diagrams, and multimedia presentations.

CLASSIFYING Classifying objects is grouping them according to how they are similar, how they are different, or how they are related to one another. Scientists classify everything from animals to planets.

An agricultural engineer takes soil measurements.

MEASURING Scientists use tools to take precise measurements of what they observe. Tools measure things like temperature, mass, distance, volume, and time.

INFERRING Inferring means using observations and what you know to figure something out. Here's an example. A scientist observes that every time a large insect comes near a smaller one, the smaller insect releases a dark, sticky liquid from its body. The larger insect flies away. If the scientist saw this many times, she could eventually figure out, or infer, that the liquid helps the smaller insect defend itself.

PREDICTING A scientist can use what he or she knows and observes to predict the outcome of an action. In the case of the small insect, a scientist could predict that the small insect would release the sticky fluid the next time a larger insect came near.

General Steps in the Scientific Method

1. QUESTION

What makes you curious? Look around and observe the world. Think about the materials you have available. What are these things made of, how do they work, and what can you do with them? What do you want to find out? Do some research online or at a library. Decide what question you want to answer.

Research a topic that interests you before you plan your experiment.

2. HYPOTHESIS

Think about how you could answer your question. Based on what you've seen and read, what do you predict will happen? What do you think the outcome of the experiment will be? Why do you think this is so? Make a prediction using an "If _____, then _____ because _____" statement format. For example, your hypothesis could be, "If I give a plant more water, then it will grow taller because plants need water to grow."

Be precise with measurements.

3. EXPERIMENT

Create a list of the materials you need. Write out each step of your experimental procedure. Carry out each step carefully. Make sure you work safely and accurately. Record what you observe with words and pictures.

4. RESULTS

What happened? Record all your results. Use graphs and charts to clearly show your findings.

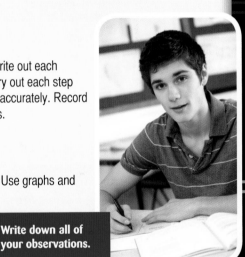

Write down all of your observations.

5. CONCLUSION

What do your results tell you? Analyze your results and compare actual results with your hypothesis. Decide whether or not your results support your hypothesis. Think about further research you could do on your topic. What new experiment ideas do you have now? Write up your findings to share with other scientists.

PLAY IT SAFE!

Remember to be safe when you do the projects in this book.

✔ Be sure safety equipment is nearby. If you are doing an experiment with heat, know where you can find a fire extinguisher.

✔ If you are going to handle something hot, use pot holders, oven mitts, or thick gloves.

✔ Read all the instructions before you begin.

✔ Do not eat or drink any parts of an experiment unless you are told to.

✔ Pull back long hair so it's out of the way.

✔ Be sure to clean up all surfaces when you're done with experiments.

✔ Wear shoes with closed toes when you are doing experiments.

✔ Get adult help with anything sharp, electric, or hot.

LIFE SCIENCE

How do plants survive in the desert? Why are some animals endangered while others are just fine? What's up with camouflage? And how does the human body work? Life science explores living things, like plants and animals (including humans). Biology is a life science that includes the study of life, from cells and genes to every kind of animal and how it evolves. Microbiology is the scientific study of microscopic organisms. Botany focuses on plants, and zoology is the study of animals.

THIRSTY PLANTS

Like you, plants cannot live without water. But when you water a plant, you pour the water onto the soil around it. How does the water get into the plant? Are there conditions that make it easier for plants to "drink"?

The Vascular System

Plants don't drink the way we do. But like us, they do need to ingest water. If you look closely at any leaf, you can see veins running through it. The veins are the plant's **vascular system**—a system of tubes that carry water and nutrients throughout the plant. In plants, there are two types of vascular tubes: phloem and xylem. **Phloem** (*flow*-em) tubes carry sugars and other nutrients the plant makes during photosynthesis to all parts of the plant. **Xylem** (*zye*-lem) tubes carry water and minerals from the roots up to the stems and leaves. Water evaporates and exits the leaf through stomata. **Stomata** are small holes in the top surface of leaves.

Similar to the vascular system in plants, humans have a cardiovascular, or circulatory, system. Its main organ is the heart. Instead of carrying water and minerals, our veins and arteries carry blood all over our body.

You can see a part of a plant's vascular system simply by looking at a leaf.

This leaf has been magnified to appear 40 times larger than its actual size. Now the stomata are easy to see.

This microscopic image shows a cross section of the root of a buttercup plant.

This is the **vascular bundle.** Tissues, such as xylem and phloem, are found inside the vascular bundle. These tissues help to support and conduct liquid around the plant.

Xylem tubes begin at the plant's roots and continue through the stems, leaves, and flowers, carrying water and minerals throughout the plant.

Plants make food during photosynthesis. This takes place mostly in the plant's leaves. **Phloem** carries food produced during photosynthesis from the leaves to all parts of the plant.

Fluid Movement in Plants

Water doesn't just flow upward through xylem on its own. It has to fight the downward force of gravity. Water is sucked upward because of transpiration. **Transpiration** is the loss of water from plants through the stomata on the surface of the leaves, mostly by evaporation. As water evaporates through the leaves, a vacuum is created at the top of the xylem tube. This vacuum pulls water up through the xylem.

Transpiration happens faster at higher air temperatures than at lower ones. Why? Because water evaporates faster as temperature increases.

Warm water also flows through xylem faster than cold water. That's because warm water is less viscous, or thick and sticky, inside the xylem tube than cold water. Think of what it's like to drink a milk shake through a straw. When the shake is cold, it is thick and harder to suck through the straw. But as the shake warms up, it gets thinner. You can pull it up through the straw more easily.

During transpiration, water leaves the plant and evaporates.

Transpiration causes a force that pulls liquid up from the ground through the xylem.

When you see droplets of water on a plant leaf, you are probably noticing dew or raindrops. Transpiration is a nearly invisible process.

A plant's roots absorb water and minerals from the soil.

A large oak tree can transpire 40,000 gallons (151,000 L) of water in a year. That's a lot of moisture being released into the atmosphere!

WATER ON THE MOVE

How does temperature affect the movement of water through plants? In this experiment, you will observe the movement of cold and warm water through two plants to see if there is a difference.

How Do Plants Drink?

YOU WILL NEED:

- Marker
- Tape
- 2 beakers
- Very warm water
- Ice-cold water
- Food coloring
- Room-temperature water
- Bowl
- 2 white carnations
- Scissors
- Watch or clock timer

science fair tip

The morning of the science fair, set out two beakers filled with water and a different color food coloring. Place a white carnation in each glass. Encourage visitors to your booth to return later in the day to see if they can detect a difference in the flowers' appearance.

1 Write "cold water" on one piece of tape and "warm water" on the other piece. Put one of the tape labels on each beaker.

2 Add ¼ cup (60 mL) of very warm water to the "warm water" beaker. Add ¼ cup (60 mL) of ice-cold water to the "cold water" beaker.

3 Add 20 drops of food coloring to each beaker to give the water a deep color. Set the beakers aside while you complete step 4.

4 Fill the bowl with room-temperature water. Place the ends of the flowers in the bowl of water. Cut the ends at an angle while keeping them underwater. The stems should be the same length, about 1 to 2 inches (3 to 5 cm) longer than the height of the beakers.

COOLING OFF, NATURALLY

Having tall trees around a house is a good thing—especially in summer. In hot weather, a house with large trees around it will be cooler than one that stands in direct sunlight. Part of the reason is the shade provided by the leafy branches. But transpiration also helps cool the house. When it's warm outside, a lot of transpiration occurs in the trees. The water vapor the trees give off helps keep the air under the treetops—and around the house—cooler than the air in direct sun.

5 Put one flower into each beaker. Record the time.

6 Draw or photograph the flowers at regular intervals for two days. Compare the colors of the flowers. What do you observe?

The SCIENCE Behind It

You just traced how plants drink. The colored water was pulled up the xylem all the way into the flowers' petals. Water evaporates out of the petals, leaving the color behind. The evaporation from the flower petals also helps pull water up the xylem in the stem. Notice how the color moves along the petal. By studying how the petals change color, you can see the xylem's structure. Think about your observations in this experiment. Based on what you saw, what statement can you make about the difference in the movement of cold water and warm water in a plant?

Water is made up of tiny particles called molecules. Water molecules move around more quickly when they are warm. This makes warm water move up the xylem faster and color the plant faster than cold water.

☞ Using several stems of the same type of plant and keeping all other conditions equal, redo the experiment at several temperatures, ranging from very cold to very hot. Observe the plants carefully, and measure the advance of the colored water in the plants' stems and leaves over time. Graph the results. Determine the best temperature for water movement in the plant.

☞ Do all plants drink water the same way? Try your experiment again with a different type of flower, or another type of plant such as celery stalks.

☞ See what happens when the water solution contains either salt or sugar.

Change it UP!

YEAST FERMENTATION

How do bakers turn a bowl of tasteless flour and water into a delicious, aromatic loaf of bread? With the aid of a tiny organism called yeast and an amazing biochemical string of events known as fermentation.

Sugar-Eating Fungi

Yeasts are living, single-celled, plantlike organisms. They are part of the fungus family, which means they're related to molds, mushrooms, and toadstools. Unlike plants, fungi do not have green leaves that contain chlorophyll, so they can't use sunlight to create their own food. Instead, yeast feeds on sugars in plants and other organisms.

It's All About Waste

There are hundreds of different kinds of yeast. Breads are made with a species called *Saccharomyces cerevisiae,* which is also known as baker's yeast. When this yeast eats sugar, it produces two waste products: alcohol and a gas called carbon dioxide. This is the yeast fermentation process—and it's why a loaf of bread is soft and plump rather than hard and flat.

BILLIONS OF LIVING CELLS

Yeasts are so small they can be seen only under a microscope. A single tablespoon of dry baker's yeast—the amount typically used to bake a loaf of bread—contains billions of individual yeast cells.

Yeast fermentation is also used to make alcoholic beverages: wine from grape juice, beer from barley grain, and hard cider from apples. In Japan, rice is fermented with yeast to make a drink called sake (*sah*-kee).

Fermentation in Action

1. The process begins when the three basic ingredients for making bread—flour, water, and baker's yeast—are mixed together to make a dough. The water causes carbohydrates to be released from the flour. Those carbohydrates contain a natural sugar called maltose.

2. As soon as the yeast "tastes" the maltose, it begins to feed on it. That kicks off the fermentation process—and the release of carbon dioxide. Because carbon dioxide is a gas, it would, if it could, rise up and escape from the bread dough. Instead, it gets captured in little spaces, or chambers, within the dough. Those chambers are created by gluten, a stretchy, sticky, threadlike substance that is formed when flour is mixed with water.

3. The stronger the gluten, the greater the number of chambers—and the more the dough rises. To strengthen the gluten, bakers repeatedly fold, press, and stretch the dough. That process is called kneading, and it can be done by hand or with a special machine.

4. Once the bread has been kneaded and the carbon dioxide is trapped in the dough, the bread is put into an oven to bake. The oven's heat causes the yeast to work even harder at producing carbon dioxide. As the carbon dioxide increases, so does the size of the air chambers. Eventually the heat kills the yeast, and the bread stops rising. The air chambers that have already formed stay in place, however. Those networks of tiny chambers give the finished bread its soft and spongy texture.

5. The other by-product of yeast fermentation—alcohol—gets burned off in the oven. But the alcohol still contributes to the final loaf of bread. Without the alcohol (and the maltose), bread would not have its special flavor and aroma.

FROM HIEROGLYPHICS TO PASTEURIZATION

Ancient Egyptian hieroglyphics contain drawings of bread ovens and beer distilleries. So we know that people have been using yeast fermentation to bake bread and brew beer for at least 5,000 years. But scientists didn't know that yeasts were living organisms until 1836. By 1860, the French chemist Louis Pasteur had figured out exactly how and why yeast ferments. He also learned that if the fermentation process went on too long, it ruined both beer and wine. Pasteur invented pasteurization (the heating of a food to a specific temperature) in order to kill yeast and stop beer and wine from turning sour. That discovery saved these industries a great deal of money. Pasteurization was later used to keep other foods—most notably, milk—from going bad and making people sick.

CAPTURING CARBON DIOXIDE

One of the by-products of yeast fermentation is carbon dioxide. Although carbon dioxide is an invisible gas, you can use a simple experiment to watch and measure its release during the fermentation process.

Why Does Bread Rise?

YOU WILL NEED:

- ■ 2 beakers
- ■ Warm (not hot) water
- ■ 2 packages of dry yeast
- ■ Dry-erase marker
- ■ 1 teaspoon of sugar
- ■ 2 clear plastic food bags
- ■ 2 rubber bands

1 Fill two clear beakers halfway with warm water.

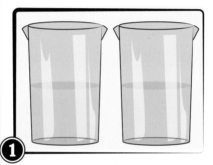

2 Stir a package of dry yeast into each beaker.

3 Mark the liquid level on each beaker with a dry-erase marker.

The little holes and air pockets you see when you look at a slice of bread are formed by gas bubbles from yeast.

A SALTY SLOWDOWN

Salt slows down the growth of yeast. Too much salt can keep yeast from fermenting and creating carbon dioxide. That's why bakers are careful about how much salt they use when making bread. They add just enough salt to the dough to make it taste good, but not too much to keep the bread from rising.

4 Add a teaspoon of sugar to one beaker and stir.

Repeat the experiment by substituting other possible yeast foods. Instead of sugar, here are some foods to try:

maple syrup	molasses	flour
honey	apple juice	salt

Do they all produce gas? Which ones create the greatest amounts of gas? Those are the ones that the yeast prefers.

5 Cover each beaker with a clear plastic bag, and secure it with a rubber band. Leave the beaker for 20–30 minutes, and observe the results.

The SCIENCE Behind It

During the process of fermentation, the yeast feeds on the sugar in the beaker, creating two by-products: alcohol and foamy bubbles of carbon dioxide. The gas then escapes from the bubbles and is captured in the plastic bag. When bread is being made, the carbon dioxide released by yeast fermentation gets trapped within the dough, causing the bread to rise.

Life Science

COLOR AND TEMPERATURE

Why do you choose certain colors for clothing? It's usually because you like the color. But are there other reasons to choose one color over another for clothing—or even the walls of a house?

When Light Strikes

When light strikes an object, one of three things happens:

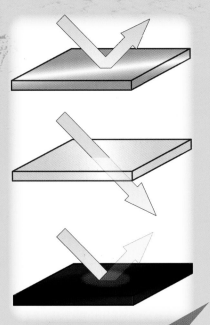

The object reflects the light. **Reflection** means the light bounces off the object. For example, a shiny surface such as a mirror reflects light.

The object transmits the light. **Transmission** means the light passes through the object. A clear object, such as a glass window, transmits light.

The object absorbs the light. **Absorption** means the object soaks up the light so that little or no light bounces off it. A dark object, such as a black asphalt road, absorbs much of the light that strikes it.

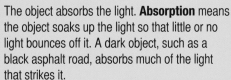

An object that is truly black would absorb all light and reflect none at all. So far, no one has been able to make an object that is totally black.

Energy Transformations

When light strikes an object that is not see-through, the object reflects some energy and absorbs some. What happens to the energy an object absorbs? That light energy is changed into heat energy. The more energy an object absorbs, the more energy it converts to heat.

Why does this happen? Light is energy in the form of electromagnetic waves. When the waves strike an object, their energy causes particles in the object to vibrate faster. This particle motion can be sensed as heat. No energy is created or destroyed when an object absorbs light energy. The energy just changes from one form to another—light to heat. The darker the color, the more light it absorbs. So, more energy becomes heat.

As the sun's electromagnetic waves strike the surface of a car, some waves bounce off. Other waves are absorbed by the car, converting the sun's energy into heat. This is what makes a car hot to the touch on a summer day.

electromagnetic waves

ENERGY CAN'T JUST DISAPPEAR

The transformation of light energy to heat energy obeys the law of conservation of energy. The law states that energy cannot be created or destroyed. But it can change from one form to another.

This principle is demonstrated on beach sand on a bright summer day. The sun's light energy strikes the sand. Some of the light energy bounces off the sand. But the sand also absorbs some of the light energy. The light energy changes into the heat that makes sand hot on a sunny day.

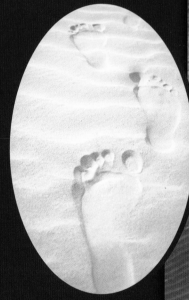

Sand will be cooler—and more pleasant to walk on—early in the morning. By the afternoon, it will have absorbed a lot of heat from the sun and can be painful for bare feet.

Life Science

YOU'RE GETTING WARMER

Some colors are cool and dark. Other colors are bright and warm. But does color really have an effect on temperature? You'll find out as you complete this experiment.

Which Warms Up Faster: A Light-Colored Liquid or a Dark One?

YOU WILL NEED:

- Cold milk
- 2 test tubes and stand
- Dark-colored food coloring
- 2 thermometers
- Pencil
- Ruler
- Graph paper
- Funnel

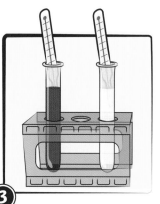

① Pour cold milk into two test tubes using the funnel.

SAFETY NOTE

Check with an adult to get permission to do this experiment. Pour the warm milk down the drain when you finish the experiment.

Time:	MILK	DARK MILK
0 Mins	40°	40°
5 Mins		
10 Mins		
15 Mins		
20 Mins		
25 Mins		
30 Mins		

④

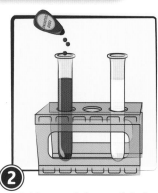

② Add several drops of dark-colored food coloring to one of the test tubes.

③ Put a thermometer into each test tube. Then record the temperature of the milk in each test tube.

Place the test tubes in the sun. Every 5 minutes for an hour, record the temperature of each test tube. What do you observe? Does one test tube of milk heat up faster than the other?

COOL HOUSES

In the past, roofs were often built with dark tiles or shingles. Some roofs were covered with thick, black tar. But as scientists, environmentalists, and people looking to save money on their energy bills have found out, roof color affects heat absorption. A white roof reflects up to 90% of the sunlight that shines on it. A black roof reflects only about 20%. As a result, white roofs keep homes cooler inside. People who live in houses with white roofs run their air conditioning less and have lower energy costs. Now, many people are painting their dark roofs white, or swapping their old, dark shingles for white tiles or shingles.

A man adds another coat of white paint to a roof in Philadelphia.

Steven Chu, the U.S. secretary of energy, has said, "Cool roofs are one of the quickest and lowest-cost ways we can reduce our global carbon emissions and begin the hard work of slowing climate change."

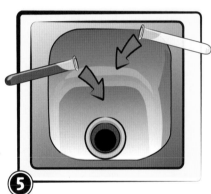

(5) Pour the warm milk down the drain.

Change it UP!

☞ Take what you've learned with liquids and test out T-shirts of different colors. Find three to five T-shirts, fold them, and set them in the sun. Place a thermometer inside each folded shirt to check the temperature. Based on your results, determine which color T-shirt would keep you coolest on a sunny day.

☞ Test the effects of different house colors on the temperatures inside them. Use identical wooden or cardboard boxes for model houses. Choose several different colors—some dark and some light—to paint the outsides. Record the change in temperature when the "houses" are left out in the sun for a couple of hours.

The SCIENCE Behind It

Light-colored objects look bright because they reflect most of the light that hits them. Dark-colored objects look dark because they absorb most of the light that hits them.

In this experiment, the darker liquid absorbed more light energy from the sun than the lighter liquid. The absorbed light energy didn't disappear. It was converted to heat energy—causing the darker liquid to heat up faster than the lighter liquid. Remember that when you are having lunch outside!

Life Science

PHYSICAL SCIENCE

How do light and sound travel? What is gravity, and why do astronauts float in space? Why do things explode? Physical science is the study of nonliving things, such as energy, matter, and magnetism. There are many branches of physical science, including chemistry, which explores chemical reactions and how elements interact, and physics, which is the study of matter, energy, forces, and how they affect one another.

ACIDS AND BASES

Many substances can be classified as acids or bases. Lemon juice is one weak acid that you know from the kitchen. Like lemon juice, most acids taste sour. A base is the opposite of an acid.

What is pH?

The value of pH is simply a way to measure how acidic or basic a liquid is. You can use pH to describe everything from shampoo to the water in a swimming pool. The value ranges from 0 to 14. Acids have pH values between 0 and 7. What are the pH values of bases? You guessed it! From 7 to 14.

Some strong acids can attack your skin and ruin your clothes. Strong bases are just as dangerous as strong acids. That's why they might irritate your skin unless you wear rubber gloves.

In the Swim of pH

The pH is important to keep a swimming pool clean and safe! The pH of our eyes is slightly basic, at 7.2. To keep a pool comfortable, the pH needs to be somewhere between 7.0–7.6. When the pool's pH is too low, acidic water can dissolve the cement or marble sides of the pool, creating places for algae to grow. Metals on the stairs and pumps could corrode, and it could make your eyes and nose burn. If the pH gets too high, you can still have problems with itchy eyes and dry skin. Swimming pool water starts to get murky.

Low pH may be the culprit if algae begin growing in a pool.

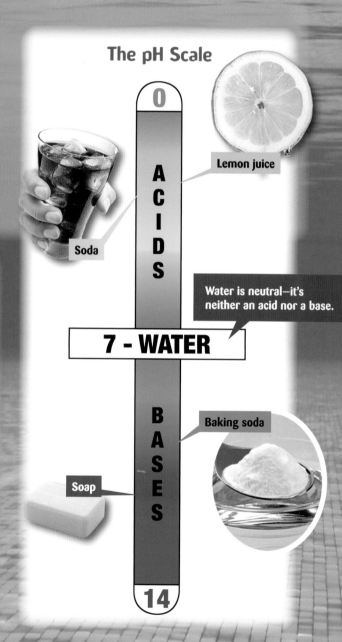

The pH Scale

0

A C I D S

Soda

Lemon juice

Water is neutral—it's neither an acid nor a base.

7 - WATER

B A S E S

Baking soda

Soap

14

How Can You Tell an Acid from a Base?

YOU WILL NEED:

- Head of red cabbage
- Medium-size bowl
- Grater
- Water
- Strainer
- Plastic container
- 3 test tubes
- Baking soda
- Test liquids: lemon juice, vinegar, cola, milk
- Beaker
- Funnel

① Use the grater (with an adult's help) to grate some red cabbage into a medium-size bowl.

② Cover the cabbage with cold water and let it sit for 45 minutes.

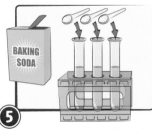

③ Strain the juice into a plastic container. Your cabbage juice indicator is ready to use.

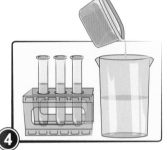

④ Test for acids. Pour an equal amount of cabbage juice into the beaker and each test tube using the funnel.

⑤ Add 1/4 teaspoon (1 mL) of baking soda to all of your test tubes. What color does it turn? The beaker, which has no baking soda, is the "control" for this experiment.

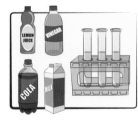

⑥ Add other substances to each test tube of cabbage juice with baking soda. What happens to the color? Can you change the juice back to its original color?

Change it UP!

☞ Repeat the experiment with Concord grape juice instead of cabbage juice. How do the cabbage and Concord grape juices compare as indicators?

The SCIENCE Behind It

The beaker, which has no baking soda, is your "control". You'll want to get your mixtures to match that color. Red cabbage juice contains chemicals that change color when mixed with certain other chemicals. Add an acid to the cabbage juice, and the cabbage juice will turn different shades of red. If you add a liquid and the juice stays blue, the liquid is probably a base, not an acid. Baking soda is a base.

CRYSTALLINE GROWTH

Some minerals, metals, and snowflakes are made up of crystals. This means that the atoms of the mineral or the ice link up in a neat, repeating pattern.

What Is a Crystal?

In some solids, the way in which the molecules and atoms build on one another can be random. But crystals are different. The atoms and molecules of a crystal repeat in an exact pattern, or uniform arrangement, over and over throughout the entire material. These patterns are symmetrical, which means they look exactly the same on one side as on the other. Because of this repetitive structure, crystals take on unique and often beautiful shapes naturally. Gemstones, such as diamonds, rubies, emeralds, and sapphires, are crystalline minerals found within and among rocks. Raw gemstones (before they are cut and polished) grow into interesting, geometric shapes with lots of angles and flat sides. Crystals' sizes vary, but if you could look at the tiniest part of the internal structure of a ruby or diamond, you would find that the mineral's atoms are connected in a neat, symmetrical, identical pattern.

Snowflakes are made up of ice crystals. Even though snowflakes have different patterns, snow crystals all have a six-sided, or hexagonal, structure.

See the difference between a raw diamond and one that has been cut and polished.

Quartz is the second most abundant mineral on Earth.

CRYSTALS IN NATURE . . . AND IN YOUR BATHTUB

Water can carry dissolved minerals into your home, too! Sometimes calcium and limestone particles will dissolve in water. Over time, these heavier minerals can get left behind on a sink or bathtub. They may look like a powdery or scummy film on the sink or tub.

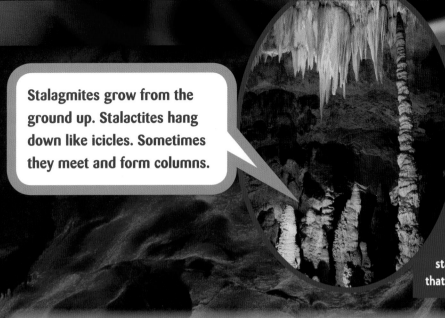

Stalagmites grow from the ground up. Stalactites hang down like icicles. Sometimes they meet and form columns.

CAVE CRYSTALS

Stalactites and stalagmites form from the dripping water inside caves. Cave water has many dissolved minerals in it, because the water has seeped through the ground and picked up dissolved materials along the way. This mineral-rich water then drips into underground caves. As the water drips and runs off, these beautiful towers of minerals are left behind. The formation of stalactites and stalagmites is a slow process that takes place over thousands of years.

Solutions, Solvents, and Solutes

When some substances mix with liquid, they break down into very tiny clusters of molecules that cannot be seen with the naked eye. We call this process **dissolving**. Even certain metals like sodium and calcium can dissolve in water. In this process, we call the liquid a **solvent,** and the material being dissolved a **solute.** Once the solute has dissolved into the solvent, we have what is called a **solution.**

Solutions look like they are only a single liquid, but they have teeny bits of material floating around in them. One way to prove that a liquid is a solution is to allow all of the liquid to evaporate. Once the liquid has dried up, the solute will reappear because solids cannot evaporate. If the solute was a crystal, it may re-form differently. Sometimes the speed at which a crystal forms changes the way its molecules are arranged, giving it a different appearance.

For example, have you ever sprinkled sugar into your drink only to watch it disappear before your eyes? Those crystals are not disappearing, they are dissolving. In other words, they are breaking down into pieces too small to see. If the liquid dries out, or evaporates, those particles reconnect and will once again be big enough to see.

Geodes are hollow rocks with crystals inside. They often form near volcanoes. Water with dissolved minerals flows into cracks and holes in the rock. Crystals slowly form inside as the water evaporates.

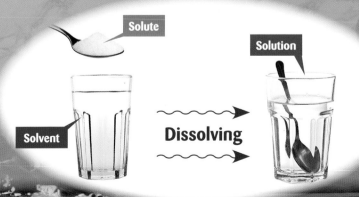

Solute

Solution

Solvent

Dissolving

ROW YOUR OWN CRYSTALS

es and stalagmites are naturally occurring crystals. But not all crystals are formed in
re. You can make your own solution and grow crystals at home.

ow Do Crystals Form?

OU WILL NEED:

- 2 beakers
- Spoon
- Salt
- Sugar
- Paintbrush
- 2 pieces of black construction paper

① Fill two beakers with warm water.

② Add a spoonful of salt to the first beaker of warm water, and stir until it dissolves.

③ Keep adding spoonfuls of salt to this beaker and stirring until no more salt will dissolve. This is your salt solution.

④ Add a spoonful of sugar to the second beaker of warm water, and stir until it dissolves.

⑤ Keep adding spoonfuls of sugar to the second beaker and stirring until no more sugar will dissolve. This is your sugar solution.

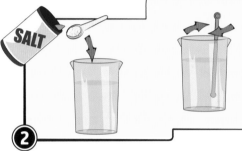

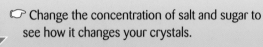

INCREDIBLE EDIBLE CRYSTALS

If you've ever eaten rock candy, then you've already eaten food made from crystallized sugar. And rock candy is easy to make at home. Just ask your parents to help, find a recipe online, and a few days later, you'll have a homemade sugary sweet treat! Some high-end cake decorators use sugar crystals to make edible decorations that look just like diamonds and other glittery jewels.

6 Use a paintbrush to draw thick lines with the salt solution on a piece of black construction paper.

7 Use a paintbrush to draw thick lines with the sugar solution on a second piece of black construction paper.

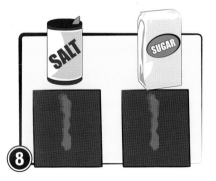

8 Allow the paper to dry, and compare the crystal formations. How are they similar or different?

Change it UP!

☞ Change the concentration of salt and sugar to see how it changes your crystals.

☞ With an adult's help, use boiling water instead of warm water. This will allow you to add even more of your solute.

☞ Compare and contrast the effects of different types of paper, such as white, colored, or glossy.

☞ What happens if you use different solutes, like baking soda, flour, or brown sugar? Do all powders create good crystals?

The SCIENCE Behind It

Crystals are made of repeating patterns of atoms or molecules. They grow best when each new crystal attaches itself to an existing crystal. When you dissolve a solid like salt in a liquid like water, the solid is called the solute and the liquid is called the solvent. You can add more solute to a hot solvent than to a cold one. As the solvent evaporates and cools, the solute comes out of the solution. The solute molecules slowly bind to each other to form crystal patterns.

Sugar comes from either sugar beets or sugarcane.

Physical Science

ALL WATER IS NOT EQUAL

Have you ever noticed that even in the middle of the coldest winters, when the ground is covered with snow and lakes have become skating rinks, the ocean doesn't turn into an enormous ice cube? That's because salt water and freshwater freeze at different temperatures.

Freezing Points and Melting Points

When a liquid gets cold enough, it goes through a phase change and becomes solid. Conversely, when a solid or frozen object gets warm enough, it will melt. Not all liquids freeze and melt at the same temperature. We call these temperatures the **freezing point** and the **melting point.** The freezing point for water is 32°F (0°C), but dissolving other materials into water can change its freezing and melting points.

The reason that the water in the oceans usually does not freeze in winter is because of the salt. Salt water has a freezing point that is much lower than freshwater's. In fact, the more salt there is in the water, the lower the freezing point of that water.

Notice how the salt water has not frozen in this wintry scene.

Icebergs are not frozen salt water, but broken pieces of glaciers that form from compacted layers of snow.

ONE-OF-A-KIND WATER

Water is unique in that it expands when it freezes. Most materials contract, or get smaller, when they freeze. Have you ever noticed that windows and doors are easier to open when it's cold outside? This is because the materials contract in winter and expand in the summer. This is also why placing a can of soda in the freezer for too long is a bad idea. Chances are, the can will explode and leave quite a mess to clean up. Want to test this safely? Put a sealed plastic water bottle in the freezer. The plastic will stretch instead of exploding.

Adding salt and other materials to water can make them boil at a higher temperature. Want your pasta to cook faster? Sprinkle a little salt in the water.

When making brownies from a mix, you may notice that the recipe calls for extra water, added flour, and/or less oil if you are cooking at elevations higher than 5,000 feet (1,524 m). That's because water boils at a lower temperature in high altitudes. If the water boils off the dessert mix too early, it may mess up the chemical reactions that take place in the oven.

Feeling Hot, Hot, Hot

Once they reach a certain temperature, some materials go through yet another phase change and become a gas. We call this temperature a **boiling point.** Air pressure can change a substance's boiling point. This is why cooking at high altitudes requires some changes to ingredients and cooking temperature.

When Will It Boil?

Here are the boiling points of some common liquids.

LIQUID	BOILING POINT	
	FAHRENHEIT	CELSIUS
◄ Acetone (nail polish remover)	133°F	56.5°C
Alcohol (rubbing alcohol)	180°F	82°C
Butane	31.1°F	-0.5°C
Iodine	363.8°F	184.3°C
Linseed oil	649.4°F	343°C
Olive oil ►	570°F	300°C
Gasoline	212–752°F	100–400°C
Propane	-44°F	-42°C
Turpentine	300–356°F	149–180°C
Water	212°F	100°C

Physical Science

CHANGING FREEZING POINTS

Can we slow down the freezing process or even keep water from freezing altogether? This experiment allows you to test the effects of salt, sugar, and other materials on water's freezing and melting points.

Can You Keep Water from Freezing?

① Fill two beakers with water.

② Label one beaker "Salt," and stir in two spoonfuls of salt.

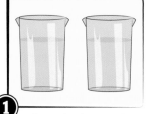

③ Label the second beaker "Sugar," and stir in two spoonfuls of sugar.

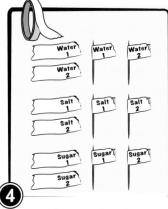

④ Write "Water 1" and "Water 2" on two small pieces of tape, and wrap each one around a toothpick, like a flag. Write "Salt 1" and "Salt 2" on two small pieces of tape, and wrap each one around a toothpick. Then write "Sugar 1" and "Sugar 2" on two small pieces of tape, and wrap each one around a toothpick.

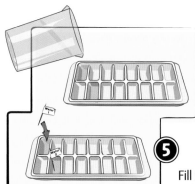

⑤ Fill two of the ice cube tray's wells with water. Do not fill two wells next to one another. Instead, always leave an empty well between the ones you fill up. Put a "water" toothpick in each well.

science fair tip

Use tape to mark a place on your counter where you will set your ice cube trays. Set up a camera on a tripod so you can take photos of the trays at the same angle each time. On your computer, create slides showing the time. Then create a slide show.

6 Fill two of the tray's wells with salt water. Put a "Salt" toothpick in each well.

7 Fill two of the tray's wells with sugar water. Put a "Sugar" toothpick in each well.

8 Put the ice cube tray in the freezer.

9 Every 30 minutes, remove the ice cube tray. Check to see which wells are frozen by trying to move the toothpicks.

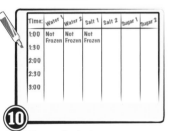

Time:	Water 1	Water 2	Salt 1	Salt 2	Sugar 1	Sugar 2
1:00	Not Frozen	Not Frozen	Not Frozen			
1:30						
2:00						
2:30						
3:00						

10 Record what you see on paper. Put the tray back into the freezer, and continue checking every 30 minutes until all the ice cubes are frozen.

11 Put the ice cube tray on the kitchen counter. Check it every 30 minutes to see which wells have thawed. Record what you see on your paper.

AMAZING ANTIFREEZE

We also use chemicals like salt to change the freezing-point temperature of snow and ice on the roads in countries that have cold winters. On snowy days, people sprinkle salt on roads and sidewalks to keep them from getting icy. Being able to change the freezing point of a liquid comes in handy in other places as well. For example, your car wouldn't be able to run if the fluid in the engine froze.

Change it UP!

☞ How would other materials affect water's freezing temperature? Try your ice cube freeze-thaw test with other materials such as:

dirt	flour
vinegar	milk
juice	pepper
baking powder	food coloring

☞ Which melts ice faster, a cup of freshwater or a cup of salt water? Thaw ice cubes to test your hypothesis.

The SCIENCE Behind It

You made antifreeze! Antifreeze is a mix of water and chemicals with very low freezing points. Water placed in a freezer loses its heat and drops in temperature. Water freezes at 32°F (0°C), but you've lowered the water's freezing point by adding salt or sugar. This means it takes the salty or sugary water longer to freeze than regular tap water. The salt or sugar also keeps the water colder, so these ice cubes thaw more slowly than the cubes made from freshwater.

Light moves faster than anything known to man. It bounces on some materials and goes right through others. Light bouncing off a highly reflective material can cook an egg. When passing through plasma and focused into a very small beam, light can become a laser and burn a hole through a piece of metal. Light can be seen in many colors or be invisible to us. Ultraviolet light is visible to some insects and birds but invisible to the human eye.

Big Waves, Little Waves

Light travels in waves. All light travels at approximately 186,282 miles (299,792 km) per second. Higher energy light, like gamma rays, travels in shorter waves, and lower energy light, like the colors of a rainbow, travels in longer waves. Regardless of how much energy the light has, it follows a straight path until it hits something. If it bounces off something rough or bumpy, the light scatters in many different directions at once. Think of carpet. Light hits the uneven surface of a carpet and then bounces in many different directions, giving the carpet the appearance of being dull. But when light bounces off something smooth like a mirror or a polished stone, the light is redirected all together, so the object looks shiny or reflective.

Light reflects off the smooth surface of the stones, making them appear shiny.

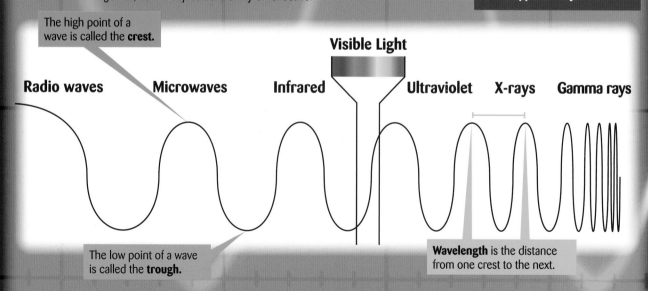

The high point of a wave is called the **crest.**

Visible Light

Radio waves   Microwaves   Infrared   Ultraviolet   X-rays   Gamma rays

The low point of a wave is called the **trough.**

Wavelength is the distance from one crest to the next.

The wavelength of a radio wave can be as big as a football field or as short as a water bottle. The wavelength of a microwave is a few inches. Gamma rays have the smallest wavelength. They are tinier than the nucleus of an atom.

Playing with Light

Light can also pass through clear materials, like glass or water, and be redirected in such a way that an object appears bigger, smaller, distorted, or even upside down. This is the function of a lens. Convex lenses are thicker in the middle, and concave lenses are thicker toward the edges.

Lenses are used in many different ways. Microscopes use lenses to magnify objects, or make them appear much bigger. The lens in a telescope can make something far away look much closer.

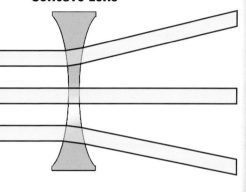

Concave Lens

Convex Lens

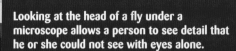

Looking at the head of a fly under a microscope allows a person to see detail that he or she could not see with eyes alone.

Both convex and concave lenses bend light rays and change the point at which they focus. Lenses are used in eyeglasses, contacts, cameras, and many other things.

LENSES HELP US EVERY DAY

Lenses can be many shapes and sizes. Humans have biconvex lenses in each of our eyes. These lenses allow us to focus on images both close to us and far away, but they also bend light in such a way that they send upside-down images to our brain. Our brain must take the information sent from our eyes and turn it right side up so that we can understand what we're looking at.

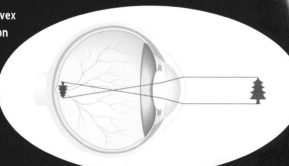

LENSES AND LIGHT

Use a drinking glass filled with water to create a homemade lens.
What happens as light travels through the lens?

Can Water Affect How Light Moves?

There are lenses in binoculars, car headlights, magnifying glasses, movie projectors, and telescopes.

1 Fold the first sheet of card stock so that it can stand up. Draw an arrow pointing to the left, and place the card behind the first beaker.

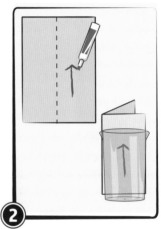

2 Fold the second sheet of card stock. Draw an arrow pointing up, and place the card behind the second beaker.

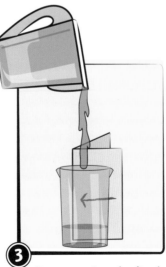

3 Pour water into the first beaker so that it fills above the arrow.

4 Look through the first beaker. Which way does the arrow point? You may need to look closely or change your viewing angle to see the effect.

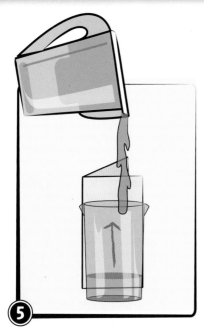

⑤ Repeat steps 3 and 4 for the second beaker. Which way does the second arrow point?

There are many ways to alter this experiment to learn more about lenses and refraction.

☞ Change the medium inside the glass. Use vinegar, honey, or soda water. Does it change the refraction?

☞ Pour your medium into a glass of a different shape. How does this change the experiment's result?

☞ Try new angles for the arrow on the paper. Which directions get flipped?

Change it UP!

The SCIENCE Behind It

You made a watery lens! Light travels in straight lines. Lenses refract, or change the direction of, a ray of light. The lens is a different medium than the air around us, which means that the lenses are made up of different material than air. Light slows down as it passes through the lens, and the direction of the light changes. Most lenses are spherical—they are rounded. Because of their shapes, they bend the light even more than a flat shape would.

In the experiment, the beaker gave your medium, the water, its shape. The water in the beaker acts as a lens. It bends the light so much that light coming in from the left bends to the right and vice versa. The result is a flipped image when you look through the beaker. The second arrow does not flip, because this lens only bends horizontal light.

LENSES OF THE FUTURE

A farsighted person suffers from hyperopia, an eye condition that makes it difficult to see objects close to the person. A nearsighted person has a condition called myopia. Things in the distance appear blurry to a nearsighted person. Scientists have created glasses and contact lenses to help people with eye conditions see more clearly.

As people age, they sometimes have trouble seeing both close up and far away. They wear bifocals, glasses that contain two different kinds of lenses in different parts of the glasses. Bifocals can be difficult to get used to and can cause headaches.

Recently, several companies have begun working with fluid-filled lenses for eyeglasses. The shape of the lenses can be changed by quickly shifting the fluid around. This enables people to alter the focus of their glasses. They can see, no matter where they are looking—all with a single pair of lenses. Another company has created a less-expensive version of these glasses, which includes dials that can be turned to adjust the level of fluid by hand. Adjustable lenses may soon be common.

SCIENCE FAIR SUCCESS SECRETS

Schools, libraries, and clubs sometimes have science fairs. What exactly is a science fair? How do you make a project for a science fair? Read on for tips on writing interesting reports and creating eye-catching displays. You'll find lots of great ideas for impressing the judges in this chapter.

SHOW WHAT YOU KNOW

Participating in a science fair is a great way to challenge yourself, to learn new things about the world around you, to practice your reasoning and writing skills, and even to meet new, interesting people. But what exactly is a science fair? And how do you make a project for a science fair?

Ask Questions

A science project is a way for you to use the same steps that scientists use to research a scientific topic. Begin with a question, like one of these: How do different sediments layer to form rocks? How does the type of soil affect plant growth? How does the air pressure in a tire affect the way a bicycle rolls? Does a truss make a bridge stronger? Which cleaning product kills the most bacteria? Once you have a question, it's time to figure out the answer.

Research

Do some background research. Why should you conduct research before beginning to work? You might find some great information to help you better understand your question and how to answer it. Research will help you make a strong prediction. The research is also important because when you put your science fair project together, you'll be able to show the groundwork that you did first. If your project is in a contest, your research will impress the judges!

State a Hypothesis

Create a hypothesis. A hypothesis is a prediction about how something works. Your hypothesis needs to be something you can test. Your hypothesis might be something like, "If I keep one plant in a closet and one on a sunny windowsill, the plant on the windowsill will grow faster." It's important in your experiment to have only one variable. In the hypothesis about plants, the variable is the location of the plant—either on the windowsill or in the closet. It's important that the plants are the same in every other way. They should have the same soil, the same amount of food and water, and start at the same height.

Observe

Plan your experiment to test your hypothesis. You should do your experiment more than one time to be sure that the results are the same each time. Take careful measurements. Use your senses, observe, use tools to measure—and record your results.

Analyze

Analyze your data. Did you get the results you expected? What did you find out? Summarize your data and draw conclusions about it.

BE ORIGINAL!

Remember, you are doing science, not just reading about it! Researching what other scientists know about your topic is important, but you also need to come up with your own experiment.

GRAPHS AND TABLES

If you have measurable results, it's important to record and present them visually, with tables and graphs. A good title describes what kind of data, or information, you collected. A table shows what your results were. A blank table is also a helpful tool when you're collecting your data. Here is an example of what a table might look like if you tested where plants grow best.

Plant Growth in Sun, Shade, and Darkness

	Carrot Top in the Sun 1	Carrot Top in the Sun 2	Carrot Top in the Shade 1	Carrot Top in the Shade 2	Carrot Top in the Dark 1	Carrot Top in the Dark 2
Day 1 height	.75 in	.75 in	.75 in	.75 in	.75 in	.75 in
Day 2 height	.75 in	.75 in	.75 in	.75 in	.75 in	.75 in
Day 3 height	1 in	.75 in	.75 in	.75 in	.75 in	.75 in
Day 4 height	1.25 in	1 in	.75 in	1 in	.75 in	.75 in
Day 5 height	1.5 in	1.25 in	.75 in	1 in	.75 in	.75 in
Day 6 height	1.75 in	1.25 in	1 in	1.25 in	.75 in	.75 in
Day 7 height	2.25 in	1.75 in	1 in	1.25 in	.75 in	.75 in
Day 8 height	2.5 in	2 in	1.25 in	1.25 in	.75 in	.75 in
Day 9 height	3 in	2.25 in	1.25 in	1.25 in	.75 in	.75 in
Day 10 height	3.25 in	3.25 in	1.25 in	1.5 in	.75 in	.75 in
Day 11 height	3.5 in	3.5 in	1.25 in	1.5 in	.75 in	.75 in
Day 12 height	4 in	4.25 in	1.5 in	1.5 in	.75 in	.75 in
Day 13 height	4.5 in	4.75 in	1.5 in	1.75 in	.75 in	.75 in
Day 14 height	5 in	5.5 in	1.75 in	2 in	.75 in	.75 in

Presenting Your Data

A graph shows the patterns or relationships you found with your data. Some common graphs include line graphs, bar graphs, and best-fit graphs. Graphs are drawn on a grid. Put the independent variable (e.g., time) along the horizontal x-axis. Put the dependent variable (e.g., height) along the vertical y-axis. Pie charts are also a useful way to show percentages. Choose a graph or chart that will best represent your results. You can draw graphs by hand, use a program like MS Excel, or search online for graph-making programs.

Bar Graphs

Bar graphs are helpful for showing how things have changed over time or for comparing different statistics. It is easy for someone to look at the data expressed on a bar graph and compare the rate of change of two or more things. In this instance, a simple bar graph helps us see how much each plant grew from the beginning of the experiment to the end. It also allows us to compare and contrast the growth of the plants in different locations.

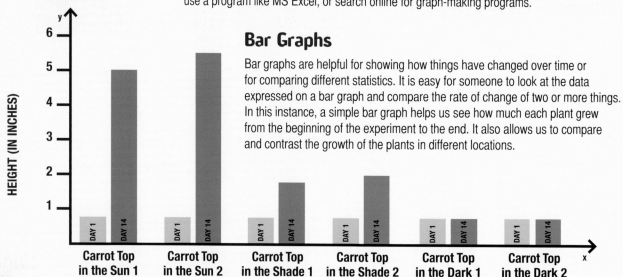

Growth of Carrot Greens over Time

Line Graphs

Creating a line graph is a simple way to display changes over time. In the line graph below, each of the carrot tops is represented by a different line. A quick glance shows us that the carrot tops in the sunny spots grew, while those in the dark did not.

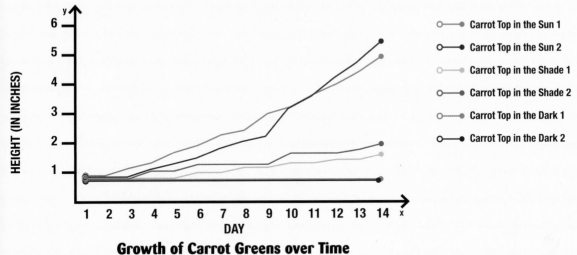

Growth of Carrot Greens over Time

X-Y Plots

You may choose to build an X-Y plot, which is also known as a scatter plot, to show how one factor affects another.

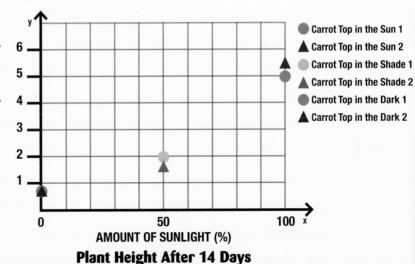

Plant Height After 14 Days

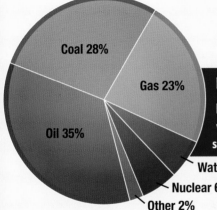

PERFECTING PIE CHARTS!

Pie charts are great for showing percentages. Unlike bar and line graphs, these visuals do not show how something changes over time. Here is an example that shows the amount of power a U.S. city gets from different sources.

SHARING YOUR PROJECT

A science fair project includes three important things: a typed report, a display, and a spoken presentation by you.

Typed Report

Your typed report stands in for you. It explains your project when you are not there. A science fair judge should be able to read your report and understand exactly what you did. This is where you put all the supporting details. Type and print your report and present it in a report cover or binder. Make sure you include headings like these in your report:

- ☞ Title
- ☞ Summary
- ☞ Question, variables, and hypothesis
- ☞ Background research
- ☞ Materials list
- ☞ Procedure
- ☞ Results
- ☞ Conclusions
- ☞ Bibliography and acknowledgements

Refer to your models and the images on your display board during your presentation to support what you are saying.

Oral Report

You may be asked to give a presentation about your experiment, or you may just need to talk about it with people and answer their questions.

Write down your key points on index cards to help you remember.

Practice explaining your experiment from beginning to end. You should be able to give a good, clear summary of what you did in about three to five minutes. You can also ask a friend to help you prepare by asking you questions about your experiment. Here are some questions you should be ready to answer:

- ☞ What is your project about?
- ☞ Why did you choose this project?
- ☞ What did you expect to accomplish?
- ☞ Did you get the answers you were looking for?
- ☞ What was your plan, how did you collect your data, and can you explain your data?
- ☞ Do you think this was the best experiment to answer your question?
- ☞ What conclusions have you come to?
- ☞ What else could you do to investigate your question?

Display samples of the materials you used or models you created. Visitors will enjoy the hands-on experience of looking at, touching, or trying out parts of your experiment.

Display

Your display summarizes your project's key points in a visual, interesting way. How you present your experiment is just as important as the experiment itself. You need to include the key headings and points from your report, and use pictures, graphs, and tables to show your procedure and results.

Science fair display boards consist of three panels and are available at most office supply stores. Choose one that is made of a sturdy material that won't bend. Use bold, clear headings for each section on your board. These headings should follow the scientific method, like your typed report. The traditional way to set up the display board looks like this, but variations are acceptable.

You may choose to put your research here, if it is short.

Make your display neat, organized, and eye-catching!

Place your typed report on the table in front of your project.

Include photos, graphs, tables, and illustrations here.

Use tables and charts to display your data. Also use photos of your results here.

You can change this layout slightly, but make sure it is easy to read from top to bottom, left to right. Your typed report should be on the table, in front of the display. You may also have equipment from your experiment set up on the table, or a model of your equipment setup. See if you can find a way to make your presentation fun and interactive!

DISPLAY TIPS

✔ Check out the rules for your science fair. Are you allowed to use demonstration equipment as part of your display? Do the judges expect your display board to be a specific size? Make sure you follow the rules!

✔ Print out your text and headings and read them before gluing them to the board. You don't want typos up there!

✔ Use glue sticks or double-sided tape to attach your headings, text, and images to the display board.

✔ Printing on thicker paper or card stock will make your board look great, and it will prevent glue ripples or bubbles in the paper.

✔ You can use colored paper to highlight or frame your text and pictures.

✔ Use a font size big enough that it can be read from a few feet away—usually that means at least a 16-point font.

✔ For headings, use a font that can be read from across a large room. You want your display to pull people in.

A SAMPLE SCIENCE EXPERIMENT: FROM BEGINNING TO END

Let's see what a science fair project looks like from the first brainstorm to the final presentation.

Question: Be Curious, but Be Practical

At the beginning of any science experiment, the scientist needs to think about what he or she is interested in. What do you want to find out? Choose a topic you find interesting, because you are going to spend a lot of time on it. Next, brainstorm ways to find answers to your questions. What materials can you use? How much time do you have? You may wonder how close to the sun a rocket can get before it melts, but that might not be the easiest experiment to carry out. Choose an interesting question that you think you can answer with the time and materials you have.

Let's say you decide to do a science fair project like the one on page 40, to see whether plants grow best in the sun, shade or dark. Once you've chosen the question you want to answer, what steps do you need to take to complete your project?

Research: Investigate and Record

Start by doing some research to find out the science behind plant growth and sunlight. Check out scientific books, magazines, and websites. Write down the useful sources and the key points you learned from each. Find some answers before you start your own investigation. What does a plant need to grow? What kinds of plant-growth experiments have other scientists done?

Begin keeping a record of your project in a notebook. This is your experiment journal. You may need to submit these notes as part of your project, so make sure you write everything clearly with dates and headings.

Hypothesis: Predict Your Outcome

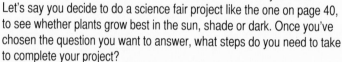

Write down the question you want to answer. In this case, "Do plants grow better in sun, shade, or darkness?" Next, write your prediction or hypothesis. Do you think the carrot tops will grow best in the sun? That means your prediction is "The carrot leaves in the sun will grow taller than those in the shade or darkness."

Experiment: Create and Follow a Step-by-Step Plan

Design the experiment. Write down your list of materials and each step of your procedure in your experiment journal. Then make sure you have all the materials you need.

Carry out your experiment, and record as much information as you can. Write, draw, measure, and photograph what you see. Measure the leaf height for each plant every day, and record your measurements in a chart. You may also want to record other observations, like how much water each plant uses. Observing everything may help you think of other experiments you can do in the future.

Analyze: What Happened and Why?

Look at your results. If the plants in the sun grow the most, then your results support your hypothesis. If the shaded plants actually grow better, your results do not support your hypothesis. That's okay! Scientists often learn more about their topic when they get unexpected results. Think about why you got these results, and write down your ideas and conclusions in your experiment journal. Maybe the sun was too hot for the plants, so the shaded plants grew better? Did your experiment raise new questions? If so, write them down and think about the experiments you could try next. To see if the hot sun had an effect, try another carrot top experiment where you test growth and temperature. You could also compare plant growth in cold, lukewarm, and very warm water.

Typed Report: Explain Your Method and Share Your Observations

Using the scientific method as your guide, type up an explanation of your experiment. Your written report needs to clearly describe the whole experiment so someone can understand it even if you are not there to explain. At the beginning of your report, include a title page and an abstract, which is a summary, or quick explanation, of the entire process in one paragraph. At the end, make sure to include a bibliography, or list of your research sources. Print the report and put it in a clean report cover or binder.

Display: Show What You Know!

Create a visual display of your plant-growth experiment on a tri-fold display board. Include the key points with eye-catching headings and colorful borders. Include a table of your measurements. Also include graphs of your results and pictures of your plants. Someone should be able to understand your experiment and your findings by looking at your display. If your science fair rules allow, you may also want to prepare a demonstration or model of your experiment. You could bring in carrot tops set up the way they were in your experiment, or a model explaining how sunlight affects plant growth.

Oral Report: Prepare a Lively, Informative Presentation

Practice and prepare so you can explain your experiment to people at the science fair. Write your key points on index cards. Practice so your presentation is interesting to listen to, and make sure you know your stuff! Be able to answer questions about what you did, why you did it, and what you learned.

Science Fair: The Big Day Has Arrived!

Bring your written report and display to the science fair and set it up at your table. Be ready to talk to everyone about what you did.

TIPS, TRICKS, AND BEST PRACTICES

How long will each step of your project take? Some experiments take a few minutes, and some take a few weeks. Write out each step of your project and how long you think it will take. Make sure you have enough time to finish and review it before the science fair!

It's a good idea to keep an experiment journal or log book when you start working. Record everything with words and pictures. Then all you need to do later to write the report is organize your notes.

You can make a new experiment by choosing a different variable to change. Some common variables to test are: heat, cold, size, shape, wetness, dryness, light, saltiness, speed, friction, weight, color, stretchiness, amount, softness, hardness, and strength. Can you think of more?

Something that can change in an experiment is called a variable. Make sure that you test only one variable at a time. For example, if you want to see if more light makes plants grow taller, light is the only variable you should change. Expose the plants to different amounts of sunlight. Everything else about the experiment has to stay the same. The plants should all be the same species and size. They should all get the same amount of water. Make sure all the plants are healthy at the beginning of your experiment. Controlling all these variables lets you be sure that light is the only thing making them grow differently.

The variable you select to change is called the "independent variable." In your results, you need to show how changing the independent variable affected things. The effects are known as the "dependent variable." For example, to see the effect that water has on growing plants, your independent variable would be the amount of water you give the plants. Your dependent variable would be the amount of growth. Your results need to show whether there is a pattern connecting these two variables. Does more water lead to more growth?

Think Like a Judge

Wondering what the judges are looking for? Most science fair judges score projects based on five big questions:

1 **DID YOU USE A SCIENTIFIC APPROACH TO THE PROBLEM?**

Follow the scientific method, and design a good test with one variable you can measure.

2 **IS THE PROJECT ORIGINAL AND CREATIVE?**

Come up with a new, interesting experiment idea, and make your display visual and exciting!

3 **IS IT THOROUGH AND ACCURATE?**

Write down all your steps and observations, and check your results twice!

4 **IS IT CLEAR?**

Write everything out and use pictures so anyone could understand your experiment, method, and observations.

5 **DID YOU LEARN FROM IT?**

Show that doing this project helped you learn something new about science.

Every science fair has its own list of rules and regulations. Make sure you read them and follow them!

SUPER SCIENCE PROJECT CHECKLIST

✔ You should change only one variable.

✔ You must control all other variables to be sure they stay the same.

✔ You should repeat the experiment at least three times to be sure your results are correct.

✔ Describe the setup of your experiment well. Draw pictures to include in your report.

✔ Think carefully as you write. Be sure to include the details of every step in your experiment.

✔ Have fun! It's exciting to conduct your own science investigations.

Image Credits